EXPLORING OUR SENSES

Touching

For a free color catalog describing Gareth Stevens' list of high-quality books, call 1-800-542-2595 (USA) or 1-800-461-9120 (Canada). Gareth Stevens' Fax: (414) 225-0377.

Library of Congress Cataloging-in-Publication Data

Pluckrose, Henry Arthur.
    Touching/by Henry Pluckrose; photographs by Chris Fairclough.
        p. cm. -- (Exploring our senses)
    Includes bibliographical references and index.
    ISBN 0-8368-1291-3
    1. Touch--Juvenile literature. [1. Touch. 2. Senses and
sensation.] I. Fairclough, Chris, ill. II. Title. III. Series.
    QP451.P583   1995
    612.8'8--dc20   94-41621

This edition first published in 1995 by
Gareth Stevens Publishing
1555 North RiverCenter Drive, Suite 201
Milwaukee, Wisconsin 53212, USA

Additional photographs: Peter Millard 14, 15.

Printed in the United States of America

1 2 3 4 5 6 7 8 9 99 98 97 96 95

EXPLORING OUR SENSES
Touching

By Henry Pluckrose
Photographs by Chris Fairclough

Gareth Stevens Publishing
MILWAUKEE

Touch a friend's hand.
How does it feel?
Is it warm or cold?

Rub your hand over this page.
Is it rough or smooth?
Hot or cold? Wet or dry?

**What do you like
to touch —
the smoothness
of wood . . .**

the roughness
of brick . . .

the grittiness
of sand . . .

or the slipperiness
of clay?

**Which do you prefer to touch —
soft things . . .**

or hard things?

Do you like to touch
the roughness of
tree bark . . .

or the smoothness of glass?

Do you like the tingle
of cold ice . . .

**or the warmth
of hot water?**

What things are
most fun to touch —
iron railings . . .

wavy cardboard . . .

sticky paint . . .

wet soap . . .

autumn leaves . . .

or smooth pebbles?

21

Have you ever felt
the sharpness of
a thorn . . .

or the prickliness
of holly . . .

the softness of feathers . . .

or the jaggedness
of rocks . . .

the smoothness
of eggshells . . .

or the roughness of terrycloth towels?

Can you imagine what
it would be like to
touch the trunk of
an elephant . . .

or the tongue
of a cat?

Touch the things around you.

What do you like touching the most? What do you like touching the least?

More Books to Read

Feel and Touch. J. Rowe and M. Perham (Childrens Press)
I Can Tell by Touching. Carolyn Otto (HarperCollins)
Touch . . . What Do You Feel? Nicholas Wood (Troll)

Videotapes

Sensing, Thinking, and Feeling. (Encyclopedia Britannica)
You and Your Five Senses. (Disney)

Activities for Learning and Fun

1. The Shape of Things to Come Can you identify cookie cutter shapes just by feeling the outlines? Put five to ten cookie cutters into a paper bag. Close your eyes and take out one of the cookie cutters. Trace the outline with your fingertips and try to identify the shape. After using your sense of touch to identify all the shapes, you can use the cutters to make delicious cookies to smell and taste!

2. The Right Touch Go on a "touch-y" scavenger hunt in your backyard or in a local park. Find something in nature that feels soft; something scratchy; something hard; something fuzzy; something smooth; and something rough. Think of other words to describe how something in nature might feel to the touch.

Index